C000180131

ANGELS

STANDING GUARD

DOUGLAS CONNELLY

8 STUDIES
FOR INDIVIDUALS
OR GROUPS

ivp

Life
Builder
Study

INTER-VARSITY PRESS
36 Causton Street, London SW1P 4ST, England
Email: ivp@ivpbooks.com
Website: www.ivpbooks.com

Originally published in the United States of America in the LifeGuide® Bible Studies series in 1995 by InterVarsity Press, Downers Grove, Illinois
Second edition published 2004
First published in Great Britain by Scripture Union in 1995
Second edition published 2004
This edition published in Great Britain by Inter-Varsity Press 2018

British Library Cataloguing-in-Publication Data
A catalogue record for this book is available from the British Library.

ISBN: 978–1–78359–788–8

Printed in Great Britain by 4edge Limited

Inter-Varsity Press publishes Christian books that are true to the Bible and that communicate the gospel, develop discipleship and strengthen the church for its mission in the world.

IVP originated within the Inter-Varsity Fellowship, now the Universities and Colleges Christian Fellowship, a student movement connecting Christian Unions in universities and colleges throughout Great Britain, and a member movement of the International Fellowship of Evangelical Students. Website: www.uccf.org.uk. That historic association is maintained, and all senior IVP staff and committee members subscribe to the UCCF Basis of Faith.

Contents

Getting the Most Out of *Angels*

In the unseen realms of God's universe, powerful and wonderful beings dwell. They move at the speed of light to carry out their master's will. They are involved in the political affairs of nations and in the smallest concerns of children. They may stand guard over your life and protect you in countless ways. They watch what goes on in the church where you worship and they engage in cosmic battles that you aren't even aware are happening. These fantastic beings are called angels.

Unfortunately, many Christians have absorbed a lot of very bad information about angels—information from some very misguided sources. Most of the resources claiming to tell us the truth about angels have explored every avenue of information except the genuine source of truth—God's Word. Angel lore, myths, ancient stories, even the experiences of people who have encountered angels must be measured against the standard of God's truth. I've written this study guide to help you discover for yourself what the Bible says about these marvelous beings.

And when you go to the Bible you won't be disappointed! Thirty-four of the Bible's sixty-six books talk about angels in detail. Every New Testament writer confirms their existence. The word *angel* occurs more than 250 times in Scripture. This is certainly no isolated truth hidden in the dark corners of the Bible! Jesus himself referred to angels as real beings who were involved in every realm of human activity. So if you have thought that angels belong in the same category as sea monsters and trolls, think again.

The Bible also makes it clear that angels fall into two distinct groups—the holy angels of God and the evil angels who followed Satan in his rebellion. Most New Age angel guides ignore that aspect of God's truth. What they don't tell you is that the angel you "get in touch with" may be out to destroy you. The best protection we have against the deception of Satan is a firm knowledge of God's Word.

We are about to embark on an exciting adventure. You will be reminded of things you have learned before, and hopefully you will learn some new truths too. My desire is that you will be open as never before to understanding and enjoying the wonderful ministry that God's angels have in your life.

Suggestions for Individual Study

1. As you begin each study, pray that God will speak to you through his Word.

2. Read the introduction to the study and respond to the personal reflection question or exercise. This is designed to help you focus on God and on the theme of the study.

3. Each study deals with a particular passage—so that you can delve into the author's meaning in that context. Read and reread the passage to be studied. The questions are written using the language of the New International Version, so you may wish to use that version of the Bible. The New Revised Standard Version is also recommended.

4. This is an inductive Bible study, designed to help you discover for yourself what Scripture is saying. The study includes three types of questions. *Observation* questions ask about the basic facts: who, what, when, where and how. *Interpretation* questions delve into the meaning of the passage. *Application* questions help you discover the implications of the text for growing in Christ. These three keys unlock the treasures of Scripture.

Write your answers to the questions in the spaces provided or in a personal journal. Writing can bring clarity and deeper understanding of yourself and of God's Word.

5. It might be good to have a Bible dictionary handy. Use it to look up any unfamiliar words, names or places.

6. Use the prayer suggestion to guide you in thanking God for what you have learned and to pray about the applications that have come to mind.

7. You may want to go on to the suggestion under "Now or Later," or you may want to use that idea for your next study.

Suggestions for Members of a Group Study

1. Come to the study prepared. Follow the suggestions for individual study mentioned above. You will find that careful preparation will greatly enrich your time spent in group discussion.

2. Be willing to participate in the discussion. The leader of your group will not be lecturing. Instead, he or she will be encouraging the members of the group to discuss what they have learned. The leader will be asking the questions that are found in this guide.

3. Stick to the topic being discussed. Your answers should be based on the verses which are the focus of the discussion and not on outside authorities such as commentaries or speakers. These studies focus on a particular passage of Scripture. Only rarely should you refer to other portions of the Bible. This allows for everyone to participate in in-depth study on equal ground.

4. Be sensitive to the other members of the group. Listen attentively when they describe what they have learned. You may be surprised by their insights! Each question assumes a variety of answers. Many questions do not have "right" answers, particularly questions that aim at meaning or application. Instead the questions push us to explore the passage more thoroughly.

When possible, link what you say to the comments of others. Also, be affirming whenever you can. This will encourage some of the more hesitant members of the group to participate.

5. Be careful not to dominate the discussion. We are sometimes so eager to express our thoughts that we leave too little opportunity for others to respond. By all means participate! But allow others to also.

6. Expect God to teach you through the passage being discussed and through the other members of the group. Pray that you will have an enjoyable and profitable time together, but also that as a result of the study you will find ways that you can take action individually and/or as a group.

7. Remember that anything said in the group is considered confidential and should not be discussed outside the group unless specific permission is given to do so.

8. If you are the group leader, you will find additional suggestions at the back of the guide.

1

Burning in God's Presence

Isaiah 6:1-7

During a particularly difficult year of my life, I experienced some profound and wonderful times of worship. Usually these came as my wife and I visited a church in our community for their midweek service. The believers began with an extended time of singing praises to the Lord. A period of prayer followed. I often sat through the whole service in tears of brokenness before God. I left in awe of the glory of God and with a transforming sense of his cleansing grace in my life.

GROUP DISCUSSION. Describe a time when you had a sense of God's close presence and glory. Where were you, and what feelings did you experience?

PERSONAL REFLECTION. What elements lead you most deeply into worship—reading the Bible, singing or listening to music, prayer? Begin this study by expressing your love and adoration to God.

The prophet Isaiah must have come to the Lord's temple with a deep sense of longing for God's presence and power. What he saw as he came in worship was a stunning vision not only of the Lord but also of magnificent angels who shouted God's praise. *Read Isaiah 6:1-7.*

1. What circumstances and personal struggles might have burdened Isaiah's heart as he came into the temple?

2. Imagine yourself in Isaiah's place. What would you tell a friend that you saw, felt, heard and smelled (vv. 1-4)?

3. Why does Isaiah have such a strong reaction to his experience (v. 5)?

4. The angel beings Isaiah saw above God's throne are called *seraphs.* The word means "burning ones." Why do you think they would be portrayed as burning?

5. What was the purpose of the coal in verses 6-7?

6. Based on Isaiah's description of the appearance, words and actions of the seraphs, what conclusions can you draw about their character?

7. How would you summarize the mission of the seraphs?

8. Consider how Isaiah must have felt as he left the temple. When have you had this kind of experience of God's holiness in worship?

9. How do you think Isaiah's personal worship was affected by this vision?

10. How will Isaiah's vision make a difference in your worship of God? (For example, does the fact that holy angels are worshiping with you give you greater confidence or make you more reluctant?)

11. What are some appropriate ways that we can acknowledge the presence of angels in our corporate worship services?

Express praise and adoration to God for his greatness and his grace. Use the words the seraphs spoke to exalt the Lord.

Now or Later

Read Revelation 5:11-12. In John's vision of heaven, millions of angels surround God's throne. What seem to be their primary functions?

You may want to conclude this study with a time of personal or group worship before the Lord. Choose one or more of the many worship hymns based on Isaiah 6 or Revelation 5. As you worship, picture the angels of God worshiping with you. Your voices join together to magnify the Lord!

2

Angels Among Us

Genesis 18:1-22; 19:1-29

Esther Maas, or Aunt Et as she is known to dozens of missionary kids around the world, was on her way to church on April 13, 1988. A short distance from home she was involved in a car accident. Almost immediately a man appeared at her van door. He took Esther's hand, and at his touch a comforting peace spread over her. The man was in his thirties, he wore tan work clothes and needed a shave. He asked one bystander to go to a nearby store and call 911. When Esther asked his name, he said he couldn't tell her his name but that she would be fine. The man stayed until the emergency crew arrived and then was gone. This man may not have been an angel, but his ministry fits with what we know from Scripture about what angelic care is like.

GROUP DISCUSSION. Imagine that you are responsible to hire a personal guardian angel. What job requirements would you list in the help-wanted ad?

PERSONAL REFLECTION. Were you ever told that you had a "guardian angel"? How would you picture such a being?

In Abraham's day social custom required that strangers be treated as honored guests. One day he met three travelers, and what Abraham discovered would change his life. *Read Genesis 18:1-22.*

1. What facts from the text demonstrate that the three men who visited Abraham appeared to be normal human travelers (18:3-5)?

2. What evidence can you find in the passage that at least one of these men was a supernatural being?

3. *Read Genesis 19:1-29.* Two of the men who visited Abraham are now specifically identified as "angels" (19:1), yet they still appear very much like human men. Describe the supernatural actions of these two angels.

4. What can you learn from their actions about the power of angels?

5. What do you think would have happened to the two angels if Lot had not taken them in?

What would have happened to Lot if he had refused to welcome them?

---

6. In God's dealings with Abraham, Lot and the people of Sodom, how do the angels demonstrate God's judgment and God's mercy?

---

7. Who in this story do you most closely identify with and why—interceding Abraham, hesitant Lot (19:16), the rescuing angels, the mocking sons-in-law (19:14) or Lot's disobedient wife (19:17, 26)?

---

8. What do these verses reveal to you about how you may experience angels?

9. How receptive are you to the intervention of angels in your life? Explain your answer.

Express your gratitude to God for creating angels as his mighty servants. Tell him that you are open to his intervention in your life —even through an angel!

Now or Later

Read Hebrews 13:2. Should we expect to encounter angels, or is this an experience limited to only a few? Explain your conclusion.

What specific actions can you take to implement this command to "entertain strangers" more fully into your life?

3

Jesus and the Angels

Hebrews 1

The people at my front door wanted to talk about a wonderful new world that was coming some day—a society marked by peace and prosperity. My questions caught them by surprise: "Who is Jesus? Is he God?"

"He's like God," they said. "He's close to God—but he is not God." I offered the biblical perspective that Jesus and God are one, but I didn't get very far. The two men walked away convinced I was wrong.

GROUP DISCUSSION. How would you explain who Jesus is to a friend who knew very little about him?

PERSONAL REFLECTION. How do you respond to people who think Jesus is just another man—a prophet or a great soul but certainly not God?

Some people in the early decades of the New Testament were having a struggle with the difference between Jesus and the angels of God. The angels had given the law of God to Moses on Mount Sinai. The angels were powerful, awesome beings. Jesus, these people said, was a great prophet, even a great angel, but not God. The writer of the book of Hebrews determined to set the record straight once and for all. As wonderful as angels are, they can't compare with Jesus. *Read Hebrews 1.*

---

1. Which of the facts about Jesus found in verses 1-3 particularly stand out to you and why?

---

2. Verses 4-5 discuss Christ's name. Several times in the Old Testament angels are called "sons of God" (see Job 1:6; 2:1 NASB). But no angel was ever given the title "Son." What is the distinction between the two titles?

---

3. What contrast does the writer draw between angels in verse 7 and the Son in verse 8?

---

4. What do the images of wind and flames of fire (v. 7) convey to you about the character and work of angels?

5. The writer of Hebrews paints a powerful picture of Jesus as the sovereign King of the universe. How does that portrait bring encouragement to you in your present circumstances?

6. What aspects of God's character are emphasized in verses 10-12?

7. How would you describe the place angels hold in God's eternal plan compared to the place Christ holds?

8. Since angels are "sent to serve those who will inherit salvation" (v. 14), would it be wrong to pray to an angel for assistance in a crisis? Explain your answer.

9. In what ways does the presence of angels as "God's ministering servants" encourage you?

10. Based on what you have learned from this study, what are some ways that holy angels might serve or minister to you that you have been unaware of?

Thank God for sending both his Son (Jesus) and his servants (angels) to help us.

Now or Later

Even though Jesus was superior to angels, several times during his ministry on earth angels ministered to him. *Read Mark 1:12-13.* What specific things could angels have done in this situation to help and encourage Jesus?

An angel also came to Jesus' aid near the end of his earthly ministry. *Read Luke 22:39-44.* How do you think an angel could have strengthened Jesus as he faced the cross?

4

Dealing with Demons

I had never had a direct confrontation with one of Satan's angels, but the man standing in front of me was definitely under demonic control. He had come into our church on a Sunday morning, but he had not come as a worshiper. A look of disdain for everything we stood for was in his eyes—and there was something more. The power of evil surrounded him. I sensed it the moment I came near him. As I walked to the front of the auditorium to begin the service, I asked the Spirit of God to block the influence of any evil spirits upon our worship. The power of God's Spirit was evident that morning as the congregation worshiped with joy and listened to God's Word with intense interest.

GROUP DISCUSSION. What person or event comes to mind when you think of evil?

PERSONAL REFLECTION. Do you think demons are active in our modern world? What leads you to that conclusion?

When Satan rebelled against the Lord and was cast down from his exalted position, a large group of angels followed him. These angels are actively pursuing Satan's agenda. Some psychologists and theologians want to dismiss demons as an ancient myth. Jesus, however, believed that demons were real. He battled with them dozens of times. *Read Mark 5:1-20.*

---

1. How would you feel if you lived near the man described in verses 1-5?

---

2. When Jesus addresses the man in verses 6-9, who responds—the man or the demons? Explain.

---

3. What can you learn from this account about the physical, emotional and spiritual oppression that people under demonic influence experience?

---

4. The demons recognized Jesus immediately even though Jesus had never been in the region. What does that tell you about the knowledge evil angels possess?

5. Would you expect demonic control to be exhibited in our culture like it was here in Mark 5? Explain how it might be displayed differently or what elements might be the same.

---

6. How would you evaluate the response of the people living in the area to Jesus' restoration of the man (vv. 14-20)?

---

7. What steps can we as Christians take to help someone who is oppressed by demonic forces?

What risks are involved in confronting demonic powers?

---

8. In your opinion can a genuine Christian be possessed like the man in the passage was? Explain to what level you believe a Christian can be "demonized."

9. Is there an area of your life in which you feel evil influences are trying to gain control? If so, how are you fighting against these influences?

10. What specific steps can you take to keep your spiritual life and focus in balance?

Thank God the Father that, in answer to Jesus' prayer, he protects us from the evil one and his angels (John 17:15).

Now or Later

Read Luke 13:10-17. What do you think were the real reasons for the synagogue ruler's reaction to this deliverance?

Based on these two incidents in Jesus' ministry, what should our response be to a person's genuine deliverance and restoration from demonic oppression?

5

The Battle Against Us

Ephesians 6:10-20

We live in a world of political crises and security alerts. Every day it seems we face some new threat. Our enemies are more than political terrorists, however. As Christians we face spiritual enemies who are out to deceive us—or destroy us. Our strength is in the protection the Lord provides.

GROUP DISCUSSION. In what life situations do you feel most at risk? When do you feel most secure?

PERSONAL REFLECTION. How do you think your friends or the people you work with would respond if you tried to explain that you as a Christian are engaged in spiritual warfare?

A spiritual battle rages in the realm of the angels. Evil powers of darkness seek to undermine us as believers. Spiritual warfare is not fantasy or a video game. It is part of every Christian's experience. If we ignore the forces arrayed against us, we are walking toward disaster. *Read Ephesians 6:10-20.*

---

1. How would you characterize the spiritual battle we are in (based particularly on vv. 12, 13 and 16)?

---

2. Why does Paul stress that we are to "put on the full armor of God" (vv. 11, 13)?

---

3. What evidence do you see of this intense spiritual struggle in your own life?

in your church?

in your nation?

---

4. Do you think every Christian is in the battle, or can a Christian choose to avoid the battle? Explain your answer.

5. Explain in your own words the meaning and importance of each piece of spiritual armor (vv. 14-17).

- Belt:

- Breastplate:

- Footwear:

- Shield:

- Helmet:

- Sword:

---

6. The word *schemes* in verse 11 implies a well-developed plan of attack. Where does Satan find it easiest to attack you?

---

7. Which piece of armor do you need to "put on" to defend yourself in your area of weakness, and what do you need to do to get that piece of armor ready for battle?

---

8. The imagery of the battle is only one description of the Christian life. It is also compared to a walk, a race, a rest and a challenging adventure. What happens to us if we see the Christian experience only as a battle?

28

What happens to us if we ignore the fact that the Christian life involves spiritual warfare?

9. Why is prayer so important in this battle (v. 18)?

10. Paul did not hesitate to ask the Ephesian Christians to pray for specific things for him (vv. 19-20). What specific requests can you share with a trusted friend or the members of your study group that will help you be more victorious in your daily battles?

Ask God to protect your life and the lives of others from the enemy's attack.

Now or Later
The angels of God are often portrayed in Scripture as the Lord's host or army. *Read 2 Kings 6:15-17.* What feelings would you have experienced in this situation if you had seen what Elisha's servant saw?

In what circumstances might we experience angel warriors fighting with us in spiritual battle?

6

Angels and Guidance

The meeting had lasted several hours. Every aspect of the decision we were facing had been debated, analyzed and discussed. All that remained was to make the decision! A long silence settled over the room. One question put everything in perspective: "How do we know if this is God's will?"

That is a question every Christian faces at times. We would be willing to make any decision, even one that would result in difficulty and sacrifice, if we just knew for certain what God's desire was.

GROUP DISCUSSION. What person or resource do you rely on most when you need advice? Give an example of when you have relied on that advice and what the results were.

PERSONAL REFLECTION. Think back to a time when you needed the Lord's guidance in a decision. How did you go about seeking his direction?

Sometimes God gives his people guidance when they aren't even seeking it. The early Christians were pretty content to keep the gospel confined within the Jewish community. What burdened God's heart, however, was the world! So God began to move his people in a totally new and unexpected direction— and God used angels to help open the door. *Read Acts 8:26-40.*

---

1. Describe both what the angel does and how Philip responds (vv. 26-28).

---

2. God sent an angel to point Philip in the direction of a seeking man. Why didn't God just send the angel directly to the eunuch?

---

3. An angel directed Philip to the road; the Spirit of God directed him to a specific person (v. 29). What distinctions can you draw between how an angel may guide a Christian and how the Spirit guides a Christian?

---

4. God obviously "sets up" this opportunity to witness about Jesus. How does that perspective help you with your fears about evangelism?

5. Imagine yourself faced with the eunuch's questions (vv. 31-35). What thoughts and feelings would you have in such a situation?

What steps can you take to grow in knowledge and faith so you will be prepared for such opportunities?

6. *Read Acts 10.* How would you characterize Cornelius's responses to God's messages?

How would you characterize Peter's responses to the messages he received?

7. An angel brought God's message to Cornelius, but the Holy Spirit spoke to Peter (vv. 19-20). When you are seeking God's guidance, should you look for an angel, listen for the Spirit's voice, or both? Explain how you came to your conclusion.

8. If a friend told you that an angel had given him or her specific guidance in a decision, how would you respond to your friend's claim?

9. Peter's visit resulted in the conversion of Cornelius's whole family. Should we look for confirming evidence of God's leading in our lives? Why or why not?

10. As the result of this study, what will you ask God for when you must make a difficult decision?

Pray that God will give you a sensitive heart to his direction in your life.

Now or Later

Read Matthew 1:20-21; 2:13, 19-20. Three times an angel appeared to Joseph in a dream. What specific details would lead Joseph to conclude that these were genuine angelic messages and not just imaginative fantasies?

Would you rather have the permanent (but quiet) leading of the Spirit in your life or the occasional (but spectacular) instruction of angels? Explain the pros and cons of each experience.

7

Guarded by Angels

Several years ago my mother visited a Christian friend of hers who was hospitalized in the intensive care unit. Her friend had been in a serious car accident and was not expected to live. When my mother came into the room one evening, her friend said, "Mary, I'm going to be okay. An angel has been sitting at the foot of my bed all day."

GROUP DISCUSSION. Describe a time when you or someone you know was protected from harm in a remarkable way.

PERSONAL REFLECTION. How would you have responded to a person who claimed that an angel had guarded her bedside? Think of a time when you were skeptical of such a claim. Then think of a time when you were more open to that kind of spiritual intervention.

One of the most wonderful ministries of angels is their protective care over believers in Jesus Christ. Usually that care is exercised in quiet, almost unnoticeable ways, but sometimes it can be astonishing. The apostle Peter learned to appreciate the protection of angels—on his way out of a locked prison! *Read Acts 12:1-17.*

---

1. What indications can you find in the text that Peter was calm even when he was under arrest?

---

2. What thoughts might have crossed Peter's mind when he was awakened by an angel (vv. 6-7)?

---

3. What do the angel's actions tell you about the nature and ministry of angels (vv. 6-11)?

---

4. Why did God send an angel—a personal being—to lead Peter out rather than just instantly removing him from the prison?

---

5. Men and women just as faithful to God as Peter have been

arrested and have died in prison. God allowed James to be executed (v. 2) but rescued Peter. Why doesn't God *always* deliver
his people?

6. Twice we are told that the Christians were praying for Peter
(vv. 5, 12). If a Christian is in danger or in trouble, should that
Christian (or his friends) ask God to send an angel for deliverance or protection? Explain your answer.

7. What strikes you as unusual about the response of the
Christians who were praying when Peter appeared at the gate
of Mary's house (vv. 12-17)?

How do you think Peter felt as he stood at the gate?

8. Based on our study of angels so far, do you think all Christians have guardian angels? Why or why not?

9. These Christians obviously were not expecting God to work like he did. In what ways do we "limit" God when we ask him to work in a particular situation?

10. How would you like for this study to expand or change your prayer life?

Thank God for his protective care over you—particularly through his holy angels.

Now or Later
Psalm 91:9-13 is a general promise to God's people of angelic protection. Read that passage carefully. What statements in these verses indicate that you and I can claim the promises of angelic care even today?

8

Discerning the Spirits

1 John 4:1-6

At the end of a seminar on angels, a woman came up to me and said that she had a wonderful angel story to tell me. It seems that this woman's best friend had a daughter who became seriously ill. The doctors were baffled about how to diagnose and treat her illness. One day as the little girl's mother was praying for God's help, she heard a weak scratching at her front door. She opened the door to find a small tabby kitten. The first thing she noticed, I was told, "was a white halo of fur around the kitten's ears." The kitten ran to the sick girl's room and jumped on the bed. The little girl was delighted and held the kitten close. Within two days the girl's symptoms had disappeared, and she was out of bed. On the third day, when the kitten was let outside in the morning, it never returned. The mother was convinced that the kitten was an angel who came to bring healing to her daughter.

As heart-warming as that story is, I have never repeated it as an account of a genuine angelic appearance. I haven't used it in that way for one simple reason. The story does not harmonize with what I read in the Bible about angels. In Scripture angels never appear to human beings as animals.

GROUP DISCUSSION. On a scale of one to ten, with one referring to a complete skeptic and ten referring to someone who completely accepts what other people say, where would you rank yourself when it comes to believing the accounts people tell of extraordinary spiritual experiences? Why?

PERSONAL REFLECTION. What are some of the results of being too closed-minded to new spiritual experiences or new insights?

What are the results of openly embracing any new teaching or experience that comes along?

Evaluating the experiences of other people is difficult. We feel so judgmental. This study will help you see the vital importance of doing just that, however. To fully accept whatever you are told may be dangerous to your spiritual health! *Read 1 John 4:1-6.*

1. How would you characterize the Christians to whom John writes—too narrow-minded or too open-minded? Support your answer from these verses.

2. We are told to "test the spirits" because there are many false prophets (v. 1). What would be some examples of false prophets today?

3. What "test" does John put forth to use in determining whether a particular teaching is from God or not (vv. 2-3)?

4. John lists some other methods of recognizing falsehood in verses 4-6. Explain them in your own words.

5. What are some other practical tests that you can use to determine if a teaching or a person's experience is from God?

6. What encouragement to help us face false prophets does John give in verses 4-6?

7. Many Christians will justify a belief or an action by saying, "God told me," or "I prayed about it." In the light of these verses, is it sinful or judgmental to evaluate another Christian's experience by the standard of God's Word? Explain.

8. How should you respond to someone if his or her belief or experience contradicts the clear teaching of the Bible?

9. How should you respond if the person's belief or experience doesn't contradict Scripture but is different from your belief or experience?

10. We've come to the end of our study on these fascinating beings called angels. In what specific ways has this study changed your spiritual life?

Ask God to give you the discernment to be able to separate truth and error.

Now or Later
Read 2 Corinthians 11:13-15 and Galatians 1:8. In what ways might angels be involved in leading people away from the truth about Christ?

Imagine that your friend came to you and told you that he or she had received a message from an angel. What steps would you take to help your friend evaluate that angelic encounter?

Leader's Notes

MY GRACE IS SUFFICIENT FOR YOU. (2 COR 12:9)

Leading a Bible discussion can be an enjoyable and rewarding experience. But it can also be *scary*—especially if you've never done it before. If this is your feeling, you're in good company. When God asked Moses to lead the Israelites out of Egypt, he replied, "O Lord, please send someone else to do it!" (Ex 4:13). It was the same with Solomon, Jeremiah and Timothy, but God helped these people in spite of their weaknesses, and he will help you as well.

You don't need to be an expert on the Bible or a trained teacher to lead a Bible discussion. The idea behind these inductive studies is that the leader guides group members to discover for themselves what the Bible has to say. This method of learning will allow group members to remember much more of what is said than a lecture would.

These studies are designed to be led easily. As a matter of fact, the flow of questions through the passage from observation to interpretation to application is so natural that you may feel that the studies lead themselves. This study guide is also flexible. You can use it with a variety of groups—student, professional, neighborhood or church groups. Each study takes forty-five to sixty minutes in a group setting.

There are some important facts to know about group dynamics and encouraging discussion. The suggestions listed below should enable you to effectively and enjoyably fulfill your role as leader.

Preparing for the Study

1. Ask God to help you understand and apply the passage in your own life. Unless this happens, you will not be prepared to lead others. Pray too for the various members of the group. Ask God to open your hearts to the message of his Word and motivate you to action.

2. Read the introduction to the entire guide to get an overview of the entire book and the issues which will be explored.

3. As you begin each study, read and reread the assigned Bible passage to familiarize yourself with it.

4. This study guide is based on the New International Version of the Bible. It will help you and the group if you use this translation as the basis for your study and discussion.

5. Carefully work through each question in the study. Spend time in meditation and reflection as you consider how to respond.

6. Write your thoughts and responses in the space provided in the study guide. This will help you to express your understanding of the passage clearly.

7. It might help to have a Bible dictionary handy. Use it to look up any unfamiliar words, names or places. (For additional help on how to study a passage, see chapter five of *How to Lead a LifeBuilder Study*, IVP, 2018.)

8. Consider how you can apply the Scripture to your life. Remember that the group will follow your lead in responding to the studies. They will not go any deeper than you do.

9. Once you have finished your own study of the passage, familiarize yourself with the leader's notes for the study you are leading. These are designed to help you in several ways. First, they tell you the purpose the study guide author had in mind when writing the study. Take time to think through how the study questions work together to accomplish that purpose. Second, the notes provide you with additional background information or suggestions on group dynamics for various questions. This information can be useful when people have difficulty understanding or answering a question. Third, the leader's notes can alert you to potential problems you may encounter during the study.

10. If you wish to remind yourself of anything mentioned in the leader's notes, make a note to yourself below that question in the study.

Leading the Study

1. Begin the study on time. Open with prayer, asking God to help the group to understand and apply the passage.

2. Be sure that everyone in your group has a study guide. Encourage the group to prepare beforehand for each discussion by reading the introduction to the guide and by working through the questions in the study.

3. At the beginning of your first time together, explain that these studies are meant to be discussions, not lectures. Encourage the members of the group to participate. However, do not put pressure on those who may be hesitant to speak during the first few sessions. You may want to suggest the following guidelines to your group.

☐ Stick to the topic being discussed.

☐ Your responses should be based on the verses which are the focus of the discussion and not on outside authorities such as commentaries or speakers.

☐ These studies focus on a particular passage of Scripture. Only rarely should you refer to other portions of the Bible. This allows for everyone to participate in in-depth study on equal ground.

☐ Anything said in the group is considered confidential and will not be discussed outside the group unless specific permission is given to do so.

☐ We will listen attentively to each other and provide time for each person present to talk.

☐ We will pray for each other.

4. Have a group member read the introduction at the beginning of the discussion.

5. Every session begins with a group discussion question. The question or activity is meant to be used before the passage is read. The question introduces the theme of the study and encourages group members to begin to open up. Encourage as many members as possible to participate, and be ready to get the discussion going with your own response.

This section is designed to reveal where our thoughts or feelings need to be transformed by Scripture. That is why it is especially important not to read the passage before the discussion question is asked. The passage will tend to color the honest reactions people would otherwise give because they are, of course, supposed to think the way the Bible does.

You may want to supplement the group discussion question with an icebreaker to help people to get comfortable. See the community section of the *Small Group Starter Kit* (IVP, 1995) for more ideas.

You also might want to use the personal reflection question with your group. Either allow a time of silence for people to respond individually or discuss it together.

6. Have a group member (or members if the passage is long) read aloud the passage to be studied. Then give people several minutes to read the passage again silently so that they can take it all in.

7. Question 1 will generally be an overview question designed to briefly survey the passage. Encourage the group to look at the whole passage, but try to avoid getting sidetracked by questions or issues that will be addressed later in the study.

8. As you ask the questions, keep in mind that they are designed to be used just as they are written. You may simply read them aloud. Or you may prefer to express them in your own words.

There may be times when it is appropriate to deviate from the study guide. For example, a question may have already been answered. If so, move on to the next question. Or someone may raise an important question not covered in the guide. Take time to discuss it, but try to keep the group from going off on tangents.

9. Avoid answering your own questions. If necessary, repeat or rephrase them until they are clearly understood. Or point out something you read in the leader's notes to clarify the context or meaning. An eager group quickly becomes passive and silent if they think the leader will do most of the talking.

10. Don't be afraid of silence. People may need time to think about the question before formulating their answers.

11. Don't be content with just one answer. Ask, "What do the rest of you think?" or "Anything else?" until several people have given answers to the question.

12. Acknowledge all contributions. Try to be affirming whenever possible. Never reject an answer. If it is clearly off-base, ask, "Which verse led you to that conclusion?" or again, "What do the rest of you think?"

13. Don't expect every answer to be addressed to you, even though this will probably happen at first. As group members become more at ease, they will begin to truly interact with each other. This is one sign of healthy discussion.

14. Don't be afraid of controversy. It can be very stimulating. If you don't resolve an issue completely, don't be frustrated. Move on and keep it in mind for later. A subsequent study may solve the problem.

15. Periodically summarize what the group has said about the passage. This helps to draw together the various ideas mentioned and gives continuity to the study. But don't preach.

16. At the end of the Bible discussion you may want to allow group members a time of quiet to work on an idea under "Now or Later." Then discuss what you experienced. Or you may want to encourage group members to work on these ideas between meetings. Give an opportunity during the session for people to talk about what they are learning.

17. Conclude your time together with conversational prayer, adapting the prayer suggestion at the end of the study to your group. Ask for God's help in following through on the commitments you've made.

18. End on time.

Many more suggestions and helps are found in *How to Lead a LifeBuilder Study.*

Components of Small Groups

A healthy small group should do more than study the Bible. There are four components to consider as you structure your time together.

Nurture. Small groups help us to grow in our knowledge and love of God. Bible study is the key to making this happen and is the foundation of your small group.

Community. Small groups are a great place to develop deep friendships with other Christians. Allow time for informal interaction before and after each study. Plan activities and games that will help you get to know each other. Spend time having fun together—going on a picnic or cooking dinner together.

Worship and prayer. Your study will be enhanced by spending time praising God together in prayer or song. Pray for each other's needs—and keep track of how God is answering prayer in your group. Ask God to help you to apply what you are learning in your study.

Outreach. Reaching out to others can be a practical way of applying what you are learning, and it will keep your group from becoming self-focused. Host a series of evangelistic discussions for your friends or neighbors. Clean up the yard of an elderly friend. Serve at a soup kitchen together, or spend a day working in the community.

Many more suggestions and helps in each of these areas are found in the *Small Group Starter Kit.* You will also find information on building a small group. Reading through the starter kit will be worth your time.

General introduction. It might be helpful for you as a leader to prepare for this study by reading a biblical survey of the ministry of angels. Not every book—not even every Christian book—on angels can be trusted. Always compare what you read with the teachings of Scripture.

You can find a survey on angels in most systematic theology books. Your pastor or spiritual leader should be able to direct you to a reliable one. I would recommend C. Fred Dickason, *Angels: Elect and Evil* (Chicago: Moody Press, 1997) as a good place to start.

As a leader you will have to exercise particular care throughout this study to evaluate the personal experiences of individuals. Many people believe they have had an encounter with an angel and have told their stories in widely read books or on talk shows. These experiences need to be compared carefully with the teachings of the Bible.

Two key principles will guide you. First, it is not wrong or unspiritual to lovingly evaluate the experiences of another person, even of another Christian. The apostle John commanded us to "test the spirits," not to trust the spirits. Second, the key to evaluating another person's or even our own experiences is the Word of God. Measure what a person says about an angel encounter against God's truth. Whatever is in harmony with what we find in Scripture, we can accept. Whatever contradicts the teaching or the spirit of the Bible must be questioned or rejected. Your responsibility as the discussion leader will be to return the group to the clear teaching of the Bible as the only reliable source of truth in the realm of angels.

Study 1. Burning in God's Presence. Isaiah 6:1-7.

Purpose: To introduce the primary function of angels as the servants of God.

Question 1. Isaiah's vision of the Lord came after the death of the godly king Uzziah in 740 B.C. Uzziah had ruled in righteous obedience to God until, in an act of pride, he tried to take the place of the priests by burning incense in the temple. He was struck with leprosy and lived as an outcast until his death (2 Chron 26:16-21). Uzziah is also called Azariah (2 Kings 14:21). Uzziah's death may have left Isaiah in a state of uncertainly about the nation's future and even his own future. He came to God's earthly temple seeking comfort and was given a vision of the sovereign King sitting in the heavenly temple.

Question 2. Don't forget to mention the shaking of the temple and the sweet smoke of incense (v. 4).

Question 3. The purity and majesty of God revealed how far short of God's perfection Isaiah fell. It also exposed the corruption of the society in which he lived. The closer we move toward the light of God's holiness, the more our own need is revealed.

Question 4. Early church theologians wrestled for a long time over the exact ranking and order of the angels. Thomas Aquinas finally settled on a nine-level hierarchy. According to his scheme, the seraphs were the highest and most powerful angels, who dwelt closest to the presence of God. They "burned" with God's holy brilliance! You will sometimes hear or read these angels referred to as *seraphim*. In the Hebrew language, adding *im* to a noun makes it plural in form.

Question 5. The seraphs became agents of God's purifying power as one of the seraphs touched Isaiah's lips with a burning coal in an act of consecration.

Question 6. It is important to emphasize that these angelic beings are personal beings. They have intelligence (to see and respond to God's glory); they have a will (to act obediently to God's direction); they have the ability to speak (in praise to God and in communication with Isaiah). God created the angels as unique, personal beings who are able to relate to the other category of created personal beings—human beings—and to God (who is also a person).

Question 7. The primary functions of the seraphs are to stand or fly above God's throne and to continually declare God's holiness. They exist simply to attribute worth to God by announcing the perfection of his character. These powerful, majestic beings are perfectly fulfilled doing nothing other than worshiping the eternal God!

Question 10. We as believers should recognize that when we worship God either individually or corporately, we are not alone. Angels worship continually before God's throne.

Question 11. The angels are very interested in our corporate services and in the work of the local church. See, for example, 1 Timothy 5:21 and 1 Corinthians 11:10. Some suggestions for acknowledging the presence of angels are (1) to use Scripture readings or affirmations of faith which include references to God's angels, (2) to select hymns which point out the fact that angels are present with us to worship God or (3) to teach passages of Scripture that declare the truth about angels. Angels are never to be worshiped but are worshipers with us of the true and living God.

Now or Later. John is ushered into God's throne room at a crucial point in the history of our redemption. Millions of angels are gathered to see the beginning of God's final work of reclaiming his creation. These angels focus on worship and praise. They express verbally the wonders of God's character. That is exactly what worship is, whether it comes from a human believer or from an angel servant.

The purpose of concluding the study with worship is to give the members of the group the opportunity to praise God along with the angels. The recent rise in the popularity of angels has led some people to unbiblical extremes. We are never to worship or pray to angels. Holy angels are pictured in the Bible as servants of God. They come to our aid at God's command, not because we call them (see Ps 103:20).

Study 2. Angels Among Us. Genesis 18:1-22; 19:1-29.

Purpose: To discover how angels appear to human beings in the Bible, and to consider whether that is still a possibility today.

Question 1. Some key indicators that these men appeared to be normal human beings may be overlooked on the first reading of the passage. The travelers had feet that could be washed (18:4); they ate human food (18:5); they spoke human language (18:5). Apparently no angel wings were folded under their robes!

Question 2. One of the "men" who visited Abraham is called "the Lord" (18:1, 10, 13, 17, 20, 22). He also displayed attributes of deity. He knew what Sarah did and thought in secret (18:13); he claimed divine power (18:14); he was able to predict the future with certainty (18:14).

Question 5. Lot's offer of his daughters to the men of Sodom was certainly not an action of which the Lord (or the angels) approved. Lot realized the importance of protecting his guests, but he spoke out of desperation. The angels protected both Lot and his daughters. Lot's tendency to act foolishly in a crisis was picked up by his daughters, who later seduced their own father (Gen 19:30-38).

Question 6. The rescue of Lot and the destruction of Sodom became a common illustration of God's ability to rescue the righteous and to punish the wicked. See 2 Peter 2:6-9 and Jude 7; also Deuteronomy 29:23; Isaiah 1:9; 13:19; Jeremiah 50:40; Amos 4:11.

Question 7. Lot's wife became a proverbial warning to later generations (see Lk 17:32). Even today, large, weirdly shaped salt formations at the southern end of the Dead Sea are reminders of her desire to cling to the old lifestyle even as it was in the process of being destroyed.

Question 8. Keep in mind that direct angelic encounters are rare in the biblical narrative. Not every Christian will have a visit from an angel. We aren't to initiate contact with angels as some "angel guides" suggest, but we can certainly be open to their presence and (possibly) their intervention.

Question 9. Some members of the group may *not* want an angel encounter! Explore their concerns and fears. Don't assume that an angel's appearance is a comforting experience. Usually the first thing an angel says to a startled human is, "Don't be afraid."

Now or Later. Some Bible scholars believe that the writer of Hebrews was referring back to Abraham and Lot and their angelic visitors and not to the possibility of angels visiting believers today. That interpretation in my mind is too limited. As I read the passage, the writer clearly opens the door to the possibility that angels may at times enter into the human realm for our blessing.

Study 3. Jesus and the Angels. Hebrews 1.

Purpose: To demonstrate the superiority of Jesus, God's Son, over the angels, God's servants.

Group discussion. Encourage the group to think of a variety of answers, but be careful that the discussion on this question does not consume the entire study time. The purpose of the question is to focus attention on Jesus as God the Son and our Savior.

Question 1. At least seven declarations about Jesus appear in these verses: (1) He is the Father's appointed heir. All authority has been entrusted to Jesus (Mt 28:18). (2) He is the Creator (Col 1:16). (3) Jesus is the outshining of God's glory. When we look at Jesus, we see the invisible God made visible (Col 1:15). (4) He is the exact representation of God—not a godly reflection or a godlike being but God himself. (5) Jesus sustains the universe by his power. (6) He provided the means for us to be cleansed from sin by his death on the cross. (7) He is seated at the Father's right hand. The work of redemption is complete and Jesus now reigns over all as Lord.

The writer of Hebrews had one objective—to declare the uniqueness of Jesus the Son. No one and nothing in any realm of creation compares with Christ.

Question 2. The writer documents Jesus' superiority over the angels by referring to seven Old Testament quotations. The angels were created as "sons of God"—a wonderful position of glory. Jesus, however, existed forever in the relationship of Son to the Father. Jesus himself called God "the Father" or "my Father"—a claim the Jewish leaders correctly understood as a claim to equality with God (Jn 10:29-30, 33).

Question 3. Hebrews 1:8 is one of the clearest New Testament declarations of the deity of Jesus. In the quotation from Psalm 45:6-7, God the Father refers to Jesus the Son as God—"Your throne, O God, will last forever." The angels are God's servants; Jesus reigns as sovereign.

Question 4. The image of wind speaks of the angels' swiftness and their secretive work. We cannot see the wind, but we certainly feel its effect. (Compare the same image used of the Holy Spirit in John 3:8.) The image of flames of fire may convey the purity of these wonderful beings. These images may also indicate that the ministries of angels are changeable like the flickering of a flame or the shifting of a breeze. Jesus, in contrast, rules in a permanent position at the Father's right hand.

Question 6. The writer's emphasis is on God's eternal and unchanging nature. The created universe will perish (v. 7), but God remains.

Question 8. Some Christians have been influenced by the New Age angel movement to believe that we should pray to or venerate angels in some way. The Scriptures are clear that we are never to worship angels. The pattern of prayer is to God the Father through God the Son in the power of God the Spirit. We are never instructed or encouraged to pray to angels or human beings.

Question 9. The fact that angels are inferior to Jesus should not discount their ministry to us. Just as they serve God (v. 7), they are also responsible to serve us under God's direction. Jesus is the focus of our worship and devotion as Christians, but we should not ignore the possibility of help from angels.

Question 10. The answers to this question may stray too far into speculation. Try to anchor the expectations of the group to the biblical examples and declarations. An angel will not take a chemistry exam for you!

Study 4. Dealing with Demons. Mark 5:1-20.
Purpose: To help us recognize both the reality of demons and the power of Christ alone to conquer them.

Question 2. The man was controlled by many demons (v. 9). They were able to control his speech and his actions and even to impart supernatural power to the man.

Question 3. Notice especially verse 5. Serving Satan is oppression, not freedom. The demons expected Jesus' judgment for their cruelty toward the man. They thought Jesus would send them to the Abyss (see Lk 8:31).

Question 4. Demons have remarkable spiritual insight! James says that the demons believe that God exists—but they certainly do not possess saving faith (Jas 2:19). The demons who controlled this man obviously knew Jesus and knew his true identity. Jesus usually told demons to be silent when they identified him publicly (see Mk 1:34). Jesus didn't want unsolicited testimony from demons even if they spoke the truth! In the situation in Mark 5, apparently only Jesus, his disciples and the tormented man were in Jesus' immediate presence, so Jesus did not command the silence of the demons.

Question 5. In our culture demonic activity will be displayed in very subtle, sophisticated ways. The highly educated person who denies God and God's presence in our world may be influenced by demonic power as much as a shaman chanting magic incantations in a primitive culture.

Question 7. Responses to this question may go from one extreme to the other. It is important to ground the group's answers in the declarations of Scripture. It would be profitable, too, to warn those in the group from excessive interest in or involvement with demons. Satan and his hosts are defeated foes, but they are not to be taken lightly. We need strong faith and spiritual maturity to face demons.

Question 8. My opinion is that a genuine believer who is indwelt by the Holy Spirit cannot at the same time be possessed by an evil spirit. Christians can, however, be demonized to varying degrees depending on their willingness to give Satan a foothold through disobedience or complacency.

Now or Later. The synagogue ruler may have been more upset that Jesus healed a woman than that he broke the religious rules by doing it on the sabbath.

Study 5. The Battle Against Us. Ephesians 6:10-20.

Purpose: To awaken us to the spiritual warfare raging around us and the resources that we have at our disposal.

Question 1. The phrases "rulers," "authorities," "powers of this dark world" and "spiritual forces of evil" convey the idea of a well-organized military campaign against us as believers. The image of fiery arrows and the command to stand our ground give us a glimpse of the offensive power thrown at us. This battle is not a mild skirmish but an intense barrage.

Question 2. The complete protection we need in the battle comes only if we take advantage of all that God provides. To leave a piece or two behind opens our life to attack.

Question 3. The enemy's assault may not be direct and open. It may also come in the cloak of personal discouragement, division in the church, coldness in worship or corruption in a nation.

Question 5. A good Bible commentary that gives insight on the equipment of the Roman soldier will help you draw out the purpose of each piece of armor. One good resource is Craig Keener's *IVP Bible Background Commentary: New Testament* (Downers Grove, IL.: InterVarsity Press, 2014). Be sure to apply the description of each piece to its function in the *spiritual* battle.

Question 8. Christians who see their lives only as a battle become fearful and defensive. Everything that happens is a demonic attack. Christians who ignore the battle find themselves under attack with no understanding of what is happening and no defense in place to cover their hearts and minds.

Question 10. Prayer for each other highlights the importance of standing together in battle formation. By himself a Roman soldier was vulnerable, but drawn together as a unit the army became almost invincible.

Study 6. Angels and Guidance. Acts 8:26-40; 10:1-48.

Purpose: To demonstrate how God may use angels to bring direction to his people and to compare that angelic work with the Holy Spirit's ministry of guidance.

Question 1. Male governmental bureaucrats who had access to the queen or to the king's harem were sometimes surgically castrated. A eunuch (pronounced **you**-nick) was often a well-educated slave. Eunuchs in the ancient world often held positions of significant authority and amassed great wealth for themselves. This eunuch was a convert to Judaism. He served the queen-mother of Ethiopia, whose traditional title was Candace. The Candace directed the affairs of the state for her son. The king himself was considered too sacred to pursue such earthly, mundane activities.

Question 2. God has entrusted the proclamation of the gospel to human beings. One reason is that angels can never fully know what redemption is all about (1 Pet 1:12). Only men and women who have personally tasted the Lord's goodness can share the message of salvation with passion. In his own wise plan, God has chosen what appears to us to be a foolish method (proclamation) and weak vessels (us) to do the hardest task: telling the world about Christ (1 Cor 1:25, 27).

Question 3. The ministry of angels is primarily external, while the Spirit's ministry is internal. Angels focus on the physical realm as they guard our bodies and direct our pathway. The Spirit focuses on the spiritual realm as he guards our spirits and leads us in the right way. This comparison is expanded in Dickason's *Angels: Elect and Evil*, p. 101.

Question 4. The Lord uses a prepared man (Philip) to lead another prepared man (the eunuch) to faith. We can be confident that if we are willing to be used, God will lead us to people who are ready to listen to the message of salvation.

Question 7. Angels are a poor substitute for the Holy Spirit!

God certainly *can* use angels to give us direction, but his preferred method of guidance is the voice of the Spirit within us.

Question 9. At times God may lead us into difficult situations to help us mature. Jesus was led by the Spirit into the wilderness to be tested by Satan (Mt 4:1). Objective confirmation of a decision prompted by the Lord may never come. In those situations we simply have to trust the One who sent us.

Now or Later. The angel's messages were specific and were focused directly on the issues Joseph was facing. Furthermore, the angel's instructions were based on reasons that Joseph had no way of knowing personally. For example, the angel told him to flee to Egypt because Herod would try to kill Jesus. Herod's plan was a secret (except to God), but Herod's murderous reputation made it a believable possibility.

Study 7. Guarded by Angels. Acts 12:1-17.

Purpose: To explore what the Bible teaches about the protective care of angels.

Group discussion. Responses to this question do not have to include the intervention of an angel; any story of protection will open the way into this text.

Question 1. King Herod in verse 1 is Herod Agrippa I. He was the grandson of Herod the Great, who had tried to murder the infant Jesus. Since A.D. 41, Herod Agrippa had ruled Judea and Jerusalem as a vassal king of Rome.

James (v. 2) was the first apostle to be martyred. This James was the brother of John and the son of Zebedee. He is to be distinguished from the James who later led the Jerusalem church and who (probably) wrote the New Testament book of James. The events in Acts 12 took place about ten years after Jesus' death and resurrection.

Question 4. God obviously could have supernaturally transported Peter out of prison. The personal angel was sent to bring a sense of comfort to Peter. The deliverance also became a dramatic demonstration of God's power through his holy angels.

Question 5. The only final answer to this question is that God is in control of life's situations, and God always does what is right. We may not understand his ways, but we can trust him and his love completely.

Question 6. You will get many opinions on this question. Try to balance an anticipation of God's intervention with a willingness to believe in God's goodness even if he chooses not to intervene.

Question 7. The popular belief in the days of the New Testament was that a person's "guardian angel" looked exactly like the person he protected. These Christians apparently believed that Peter had been executed and his angel had come to give them the news. It makes you wonder exactly what they had been praying for!

Question 8. We have only hints in Scripture about the protective care of angels, but the hints all point to the presence of guardian angels. In this area (as in so many other questions about angels) we cannot speak with absolute certainty. We can go as far as the Scriptures take us but no farther.

Question 9. Sometimes we think we can help God out by telling him exactly how to answer our prayers. God usually works in totally unexpected ways for his own glory.

Now or Later. The promise is to those who make the Lord their refuge. Satan tried to use this verse to tempt Jesus to jump from the highest point of the temple (see Mt 4:5-7). Jesus' response was that we are foolish to presume upon God's protection just because the devil dares us.

Study 8. Discerning the Spirits. 1 John 4:1-6.

Purpose: To help us evaluate spiritual experiences and angelic encounters according to God's truth.

Question 1. These Christians seem to be too willing to accept the testimony of anyone claiming to speak from God. John exhorts them to "test the spirits," meaning to put the claims of Christian teachers to the test. This theme is repeated in John's other letters (2 Jn 7-11; 3 Jn 4, 11). The believers at Berea were commended for laying the teaching of Paul alongside the measuring stick of God's Word to see if Paul's proclamation was true (Acts 17:11).

Question 2. Do not let the discussion become a "bashing" session against people with whom members of the group disagree. Try to focus on issues rather than personalities.

Question 3. One crucial "test" of a person who claims to speak from God is doctrine. The key doctrinal concept in John's mind is a person's view of Jesus Christ. Belief that "Jesus Christ has come in the flesh" involves that whole biblical teaching on who Jesus is. John's implication is that teachers who claim to expound God's truth must acknowledge that God the Son has come into space and time by means of the incarnation. If God has come to us in human flesh, we would expect his conception and birth to be miraculous (the virgin birth). We would expect his teaching to have the authority of God himself and to be accompanied by supernatural acts of power. We would expect his death to have an eternal purpose and we would expect the powerful testimony of the resurrection to be the climax of his ministry. For John, the test question to ask any spiritual teacher is: "What is your view of Jesus Christ?" If that teacher agrees with the Bible's declaration of who Jesus is, the teacher is from God. If the teacher denies any part of that pivotal truth, he or she is preaching a false Christ and should not be accepted.

Question 4. John's sharp contrast between truth and error is repeated in verses 4-6. "The one who is in the world" is a reference to Satan and to the worldview fostered by Satan that opposes Christ ("the spirit of the antichrist," v. 3). Christians can count on the fact that when we align ourselves with the truth of God's Word, we will find ourselves in direct opposition to the popular worldview. The solution is not, however, to pull into evangelical fortresses but to stand courageously for God's truth in the middle of a culture dominated by the spirit of the antichrist.

Question 5. Other tests might be moral (Does the teacher's lifestyle conform to biblical standards of purity and Christlikeness?) or based on love (Does this person demonstrate genuine love for believers in his or her attitude and actions?).

Question 7. Someone will probably raise Jesus' injunction in Matthew 7:1 about judging others. There is a difference, however, between self-righteous or hypocritical judgment (which Jesus condemns) and a proper judgment on truth and error. Jesus himself in the same context of Matthew 7 tells his followers to "watch out for false prophets" (7:15). The apostle Paul admonishes Christians to "test everything" (1 Thess 5:21). That judgment between truth and error and between good and evil is essential for our spiritual survival.

Question 8. Paul warns Christians to hold fast to the truth of the gospel even if they receive a different message from (what appears to be) a glorious angel. Even angelic messages are to be evaluated according to the clear declaration of God's truth in the Scriptures.

Try to get the group to map out a practical strategy for confronting false teaching and false teachers with courage and also with humility and love. If a false or cultic teaching is prominent in your area or on your campus, you may want to do some role-play activities to model Christlike confrontation.

Question 9. We need to recognize that genuine Christians have differences of opinion and practice. When the Scriptures do not speak conclusively on an issue, we are to give our brothers and sisters freedom to follow the Spirit's direction. We may not be persuaded to agree with them but we are to continue in our love for them.

Douglas Connelly is the senior pastor at Davison Missionary Church, near Flint, Michigan. He is also the author of Angels Around Us *(InterVarsity Press) and* The Bible for Blockheads *(Zondervan) as well as seventeen LifeBuilder Bible Studies.*